Shy
Stan

by **Katie Dale**
illustrated by **Diego Vaisberg**

"Children, meet Ben!" said Miss Fish.

"And this is Stan," said Ben.

"I cannot see Stan!" said Sal.

"Stan is shy," said Ben.

"Sit with us, Ben!" said Sal.

"No," said Ben. "I must sit

with Stan. He is shy."

"Can I sit with you and Stan?" said Sal.

Ben nodded.

Sal painted a big fish.

Ben painted a little shell.

It was fun.

But Stan did not paint. He was too shy.

"Sing with us, Ben!" said Tom.

"No," said Ben.

"I must sit with Stan. He is shy."

"Can I sing with you and Stan?"

said Tom. Ben nodded.

Tom sang a song.

Ben sang a bit too.

It was fun.

But Stan did not sing.

He was still shy.

"Come and play, Ben!" said Kim.

"No," said Ben. "I must play
with Stan. He is shy."

"Stan can play too," said Sal.

"We can play hide and seek!"

Ben nodded.

They all hid.

"I see Ben!" said Kim.

Hide and seek was fun.

"I see Sal," said Ben. "I see Tom!

I like hide and seek!"

"I win!" said Tom.

"No," Ben said. "Stan is still hidden."

Ben looked for Stan.

Sal looked at Kim. Kim looked at Tom.

They had never seen Stan at all.

Then...

"I see you, Stan!" said Ben.

"I win!" said Stan. "That was fun."

"Stan is not shy now!" said Ben.

They all had fun.

Quiz

1. Stan is _____?
a) Tom
b) Shy
c) Fun

2. What does Sal paint?
a) A big fish
b) A big dog
c) A little cat

3. Who asks Ben to sing?
a) Sal
b) Ben
c) Tom

4. What game do they play?

a) Hide and Seek

b) Ball

c) Tag

5. Who wins the game in the end?

a) Tom

b) Ben

c) Stan

Turn over for answers

Book Bands for Guided Reading

The Institute of Education book banding system is a scale of colours that reflects the various levels of reading difficulty. The bands are assigned by taking into account the content, the language style, the layout and phonics. Word, phrase and sentence level work is also taken into consideration.

Maverick Early Readers are a bright, attractive range of books covering the pink to white bands. All of these books have been book banded for guided reading to the industry standard and edited by a leading educational consultant.

Pink
Red
Yellow
Blue
Green
Orange
Turquoise
Purple
Gold
White

To view the whole Maverick Readers scheme, visit our website at
www.maverickearlyreaders.com

Or scan the QR code above view our scheme instantly!

Quiz Answers: 1b, 2a, 3c, 4a, 5c